NORTH
COUNTRY
NIGHT

NORTH COUNTRY NIGHT

DANIEL SAN SOUCI

DOUBLEDAY
NEW YORK LONDON TORONTO SYDNEY AUCKLAND

In memory of my father.

And a special thanks
to my wife Loretta.
—D.S.S.

Grateful acknowledgment is given to
the Lindsay Museum in Walnut Creek,
California

PUBLISHED BY DOUBLEDAY
a division of Bantam Doubleday Dell Publishing Group, Inc.
666 Fifth Avenue, New York, New York 10103

DOUBLEDAY
and the portrayal of an anchor with a dolphin
are trademarks of Doubleday,
a division of Bantam Doubleday Dell Publishing Group, Inc.

Library of Congress Cataloging-in-Publication Data

San Souci, Daniel.
North country night/by Daniel San Souci. — 1st ed.
p. cm.
Summary: Text and pictures portray the activities of woodland animals at night.
1. Nocturnal animals—Behavior—Juvenile literature.
[1. Nocturnal animals. 2. Night.] I. Title.
QL755.5.S26 1990
591.5—dc20   89-39930 CIP AC

ISBN 0-385-41319-X
ISBN 0-385-41320-3 (lib. bdg.)
RL: 3.4

Snow is falling and it's nighttime in the North Country. One by one the lights go off in the cedar-sided cabin that overlooks the deep blue lake. Now it is time for the forest to come alive with the creatures of the night.

Under the winter moon the great horned owl glides over the roof of the cabin and circles above the tops of the giant pine trees. He is searching for prey with his keen yellow eyes.

Soon the owl locates movement in the cool shadows
below the trees. A gray coyote lopes effortlessly
through the fresh snow. Although the owl is a fierce
predator, he will not disturb the coyote.

At the edge of the timber the coyote finds the tracks of a red fox. The coyote knows it would not be easy to catch the clever fox. But instinct tells him that the fox may have picked up the scent of food,

so he decides to follow the trail. The little fox is not looking for food, though. He is seeking out a woodchuck's burrow to take over for the bitter days ahead.

The coyote is not the only creature that the fox
must be aware of. Silhouetted in the moonlight,
a great tawny mountain lion is dangerously close. But

the powerful cat is preoccupied with the tracks of another animal that he is stalking. The fox is safe for now.

T he mountain lion continues stalking his prey through the dense woodland. Once the cat is at a safe distance, a porcupine lumbers into the clearing

and up to a fallen fir tree. With quills loosely attached
to his skin, this small mammal will claim the hollow
arch in the tree as his den.

After removing the last bit of snow from the entrance to his den, the porcupine crawls inside. He will stay there until the snow stops falling. Not far away a cottontail rabbit sits under a cedar tree munching on

twigs and leaves that have not been covered by the snow. Food is scarce and the rabbit has made a lucky find.

Once the cottontail has had his fill of food, he
hops along the timberline on his way to the
stream. As he starts down the embankment to the water,
he senses danger and stands frozen. Suddenly he turns

and backtracks into the woodland. At the north fork
of the black stream, a hungry bobcat has located a
rodent under a fallen bough.

Busy beavers have built a dam at the south fork of the stream. In the middle of the artificial pool that has been created, a lone beaver has picked up the

scent of the bobcat. Hurriedly he swims up to a lodge
built of twigs, mud, and logs. In this lodge he will be
safe from the sleek cat.

Downstream from the beaver lodge, a long-tailed weasel, in his white winter coat, has also picked up the bobcat's scent. The frisky little weasel, knowing

he will not fare well against the cat, paddles across the stream. He is headed for a familiar brushy area, where he can easily escape from the predator.

Just around the bend from the brush where the long-tailed weasel has taken refuge, a curious raccoon shuffles out from behind a bush. This furry scavenger

with a bandit's face makes his way down to the stream,
where he will feed at the water's edge.

The raccoon soon discovers a large rainbow trout that has washed ashore. After filling himself with the tasty fish, he continues on his journey. Across the

water, near the mouth of the lake, a wet-furred river
otter slides down an icy bank into the swift current.

While the playful otter takes another run into the
current, a mule deer trots down the embankment
to the lake's rim. The graceful deer bends her slender
neck and takes a drink of the cold water.

The mule deer turns away from the lake and makes her way toward a grove of pine trees. As dawn approaches, a soft light touches the tops of the lofty

pines. And high above in one of the trees, the great
horned owl will soon be asleep.

Across the lake and farther up the shore, the lights go on in the snow-covered cabin. In a few hours the sun will rise and chimney smoke from the breakfast hearth will signal the end of another North Country night.